DEHYDRATOR COOKBOOK
FOR BEGINNERS

Dehydrate Your Food To Extend Its Shelf Life, Preserve Its Nutrients, & Reduce Food Waste

Carole Morgan

Copyright © 2022 - All rights reserved.

Table of Contents

Introduction

Dehydration in relation to food storage can be defined as the process in which foods are preserved, through the removal or reduction of moisture. This reduction can keep the dehydrated food in healthy condition for a long period of time. Microorganisms and bacteria cannot endure reduction of moisture in food materials and therefore they are adversely reduced when foods are dehydrated.

Dehydration is also known as the process of removing water from a solid or liquid food through evaporation. The goal is to obtain a solid material that has been sufficiently water-reduced.

When compared to pre-packaged food, dehydrated food can be less expensive and lighter. This is critical for backpackers to reduce weight and save space.

This cookbook will not only teach you how to prepare delicious meals and snacks that will impress your family and guests, but it will also save you time and money because dehydrated foods are healthier and take less time and money to prepare.

This book contains recipes that are simple to prepare, nutritious, and delicious. It tells you what foods you can eat on a daily basis as well as on special occasions. Various types of food can be dried and stored for years. This book contains basic instructions for drying food in your home using a regular oven or a dehydrator.

This book also explains how to store dehydrated food and how to buy, prepare, cook, or incorporate dehydrated ingredients into dishes, meals, and recipes.

Why is Dehydration healthy?

Dehydration is healthy for consumption because of the following reasons:

1. **Retains Nutrients:** When we dehydrate foods, the nutrient in the food is our primary concern.Unlike other methods of preservation, dehydration saves the nutrients in the dehydrated food when effectively it is carried out.

2. **Bacteria free:** Dehydrated foods are germ-free. When we keep these foods for a long period oftime, they still maintain their healthy state.

3. **No Addition of External Chemicals:** The heat used to dehydrate food is the only externalrequirement for the process. This heat contains no chemicals or acids that may be dangerous for the food. Unlike some preservative methods which engage the addition of preservative chemicals, dehydration is a healthy choice for storing food.

4. **Safe Handling:** Since dehydration has nothing to do with handling dangerous chemicals orintense equipment, it is safe for the user to easily dehydrate. Dehydration can be done with the simplest household mechanical devices like oven, microwave or a dehydrator. The smoke or steam that escapes from dehydrating food is not unhealthy to the environment, unlike regular burning of waste products. This makes the process healthy.

The Fundamentals Of Dehydration

Before You Dehydrate: Requirements for Food Dehydration

Before you even think about drying your food, you need to think about a few things:

Learn a lot about your dehydrator.

When drying food, temperature, humidity, and airflow are all very important. These three things affect how good the dried food is.

Use only fresh fruits, vegetables, and meats of good quality.

Clean the food thoroughly and, as needed, remove the skin, seeds, and hull from fruits and vegetables. To allow the food to dry quickly, chop, cut, and slice it evenly.

Check that the meat is all cut the same way. Before drying, chicken, pork, turkey, game, and fish must be cut and seasoned. Pork, chicken, and fish must be smoked or cooked before being dried.

Some fruits and vegetables, such as potatoes, cauliflower, broccoli, peas, and corn, must be blanched before drying in order to retain their color, flavor, and nutrients, as well as to speed up the drying process and prevent ripening.

Apples, pears, apricots, and nectarines should not be exposed to chemical solutions such as ascorbic acid or citrus juices. Mold and bacteria cannot grow on fruits that have previously been treated with salt or sulfur.

The dehydrator can be set to different temperatures to dry fruits, vegetables, meat, or fish. Keep in mind that drying different types of food takes varying amounts of time. The temperature should be between 140 and 150 degrees Celsius.

Check to see if the food has finished cooking. When all of the water has been removed, the food will be darker, and the fruits will taste sweeter and more flavorful.

The dried food must then be completely cooled and put away immediately in containers or plastic bags that keep air out.

Below is a collection of tips to help you get the most out of your food dehydration:

Always start with good ingredients. Choose ripe, undamaged fruits and vegetables and fresh meats.

Set up your food the way you want it to be served. For example, if you want to make apple chips, you have to cut the apple into slices. You can't dry a whole apple and then cut it up.

Fruits, vegetables, and herbs should all be washed before being prepared for dehydration.

Brush fruits and vegetables with lemon juice to keep them from turning brown. You could also blanch or lightly steam the vegetables.

Ensure that your food dehydrator stays between 130°F and 140°F and that air is always moving through it.

Once your food is properly dried, put it in a container that won't let air in as soon as it has cooled. Your containers should be kept in a cool, dark place.

Check your stored food every so often to ensure it is still dry. If the food gets wet, it may go bad.

The main reason for dehydrating food is to keep it from spoiling and to extend its shelf life. Food that is less moist is unsuitable for microorganisms, which are the only things that cause decay and rotting. Proper storage protects it from heat and moisture in the air, allowing it to last longer. Food drying, also known as dehydration, is the process of removing water from food that will be stored for an extended period of time. Moisture is removed, preventing microorganisms (enzymes) that cause spoilage or decay. This extends the shelf life of seasonal fruits and vegetables. The food is dried using hot, dry air.

Preparing Vegetables and Fruits for Drying

Select a peak-season product.

A few people assume that dehydration is a method of making use of everything that has been blistered, thrashed, or have seen the best times. But actually, drying blends the taste, so continue with premier items that you are enthusiastic about chewing into.

Wash, dry, and peel.

Purchase organic and offer veggies and fruits a simple, clean, or wash, if your funds allow. That it is up to you to remove skins or not but bear in view skins are just going to get harder in texture.

Cut thinly with a small knife or mandolin.

Select pieces that are uniformly cut, around 1/8 to 1/4 inch wide, which will be dried simultaneously. Pieces will downsize as they dry, and for the outcome, including a tiny bit thicker than you wish.

Soak fruit in citrus water.

Each stage is voluntary, but only for a fruit that could be brown, such as apples and bananas. Fill a tub of equal portions of lime juice and cold water, soak in the cuts for ten minutes. Take the fruit out from the water on paper towels and pat dry.

Blanch vegetables in hot water.

This step is also optional but essential only for starchy vegetables, such as potatoes or sweet snap peas. Simmer them for several minutes, then shake to avoid the boiling in an ice bath to retain vibrant colors.

To dry optimally, it's necessary to work at an air temperature between 122/131 degrees Fahrenheit. Higher temperatures are needed for some products or to achieve the biscuit effect.

The technique is simple:

Cut the product into thick slices no more than 1 cm high, depending on the degree of moisture. In some cases, it will be enough to cut the product in half.

Place the slices on the dehydrator's baskets and place them inside the tunnel.

Select the desired temperature or program and start the dehydrator.

Store properly dried products.

How Does It Works

How Does A Dehydrator Work?

Dehydration is an old tradition that has existed since antiquity - and usually lasted for days. Thanks to today's technology, it is also very easy to keep food at home by gentle drying. In a good dehydrator, this usually only takes a few hours.

A modern dehydrator is made up of several levels where pre-cut fruits are layered. Individual pieces must have enough space and not be directly above one another. This is the only way to achieve the best drying results. The dehydrator machine works on the same principle as a conventional convection oven, but at much lower temperatures ranging from 35° C to 70° C. The air in the device is heated by a heating coil and distributed evenly by the integrated fan. The heat evaporates the water in the food, making it more durable. The resulting moisture can easily escape through the dehydrator's lid.

Dehydrators dry food sources by passing air through them at extremely low temperatures. The food items should be arranged in a single layer with no contact so that they can dry completely and uniformly. Depending on the amount of water in the food, different temperatures are suggested:

Water-thick fixings, similar to organic products, typically benefit from a higher temperature, such as 135°F, so they can dry rapidly without becoming overly fresh.

Vegetables can be dried at temperatures as low as 125°F.

Sensitive food sources, such as spices, should be dried at even lower temperatures, such as 95°F, to avoid over-drying and staining.

The USDA recommends cooking meat to an internal temperature of 165°F before drying it between 130°F and 140°F. This method is recommended to kill any potentially harmful microorganisms and encourage the cooked meat to dry out quickly and securely.

There are two types of dehydrators: Dehydrators with stacking racks and dehydrators with pullout racks are both available. The arrangement of the fan is the primary difference between these two styles; however, in our dehydrator tests, we saw insignificant difference between the two styles when we dried apple slices, parsley, and meat for jerky. We also discovered that the two styles provide models with a wide temperature and clock range, which is an important feature to look for if you want to have some control over your results with accuracy.

Dehydrators with stacked racks have a small fan at the bottom that directs air upwards. Stacking dehydrators frequently take up less space and are less expensive. Some are round, while others are more rectangular in shape; we prefer the rectangular ones because they have more surface areas and can accommodate different-shape fixings better. Stacking dehydrators are ideal for drying out novices or difficult clients.

Best Food To Dehydrate

In principle, almost all types of food can be dried in the drying machine. The most popular include:

- Fruits And Vegetables
- Fish And Meat
- Bread, Cookies And Pasta

But you can also dry herbs in the dehydrator just as effectively as mushrooms and even nuts. Make delicious, healthy snacks yourself or create your own muesli with cereals and fruits of your choice.

Fruits and vegetables are the easiest and most forgiving foods to process. Dried fruit can be eaten without rehydrating. It's a nutrient-dense food that makes an ideal snack. It can be added to oatmeal, muffins, and hot cereal to improve the nutritional quality of simple meals.

Dried vegetables are convenient for soups, stews, sauces, and dips where they can be rehydrated in the cooking process. Aromatic vegetables such as onions, garlic, carrots, celery, and peppers can be used as ingredients in meals on their own or combined into spice blends to add flavor to other dishes.

Lean meat, poultry, and fish can also be dehydrated, provided a few precautions are taken with these high-protein foods. When dehydrating, temperatures should reach 165°f (74°c) to kill any spoilage organisms. If your dehydrator doesn't go this high, place the food in the dehydrator at 145°f for at least 4 hours, until it is done. Then put it in a preheated oven at 275°f for 10 minutes so that it reaches an internal temperature of 165°f (74°c).

Cured ham can be successfully dehydrated, but pork should never be dehydrated at home or used for jerky. The temperatures used in a home dehydrator cannot destroy the trichinella parasite nor other harmful bacteria that are commonly found in pork.

Raw eggs and milk products do not dehydrate well. They are prone to bacterial contamination at dehydrating temperatures., Fatty and oily foods cannot be dried adequately in a home dehydrator. The fat won't dry properly and as a result, the food spoils quickly. This includes high-fat foods such as avocados and olives.

When dehydrating meat, you should remove all visible fat. Only lean meat, poultry, or fish should be used for dehydrating. Ground meat should be no more than 10 percent fat. Fish like salmon and mackerel have too high a fat content to make them good candidates for dehydrating; they can be dried for short-term storage, but they should not be used for long-term storage due to the increased risk of spoilage.

Foods high in sugar or alcohol won't dry properly. Foods like alcohol-soaked fruit, honey, or candy tend to absorb moisture from the air and resist dehydration.

Foods that cannot be dehydrated?

The following foods do not dehydrate well:

- **Avocados**
- **Olives**
- Lean Meats
- The potential for getting sick from eating there is not worth it.
- Milk, butter, and cheese should be avoided.
- Nuts Peanut Butter
- Carbonated Drinks

When dehydrating meat, you should remove all visible fat. Only lean meat, poultry, or fish should be used for dehydrating. Ground meat should be no more than 10 percent fat. Fish like salmon and mackerel have too high a fat content to make them good candidates for dehydrating; they can be dried for short-term storage, but they should not be used for long-term storage due to the increased risk of spoilage.

Foods high in sugar or alcohol won't dry properly. Foods like alcohol-soaked fruit, honey, or candy tend to absorb moisture from the air and resist dehydration.

Food Dehydration Procedures That Do Not Require The Use Of Specific Machinery

Sun Drying

This process is best done with fruits, which have high acid and sugar content, unlike meats and vegetables (except vine-dried beans). Meats contain high amounts of protein, which make them vulnerable to microbial growth when exposed to uncontrollable humidity and heat.

It is best to dry fruits at high temperatures, which should not go lower than 85 degrees Celsius.

Steps for Sun-drying

Choose your fruits and vegetables carefully; if you dry mediocre fruit, you will end up with a sub-par, mediocre product. Tomatoes should be rinsed and cut lengthwise into 1/6 inch thick slices, preferably large Roma tomatoes. Apricots should also be washed to remove any dirt or pesticide residue from their skin. Pitted apricots are cut into equal-sized pieces (most often in halves). When cutting apricots, tomatoes, and other dried fruits, uniformity is essential because the fruits will dry at a similar rate.

On a hot day, place the cookie sheet on the dashboard of your car, make sure the dashboard is facing the sun, place it in your backyard on a table in direct sunlight, or place it on your roof.

In the sun, tomatoes and apricots need varying lengths of time to dry. The drying duration ranges from two to four days, and the fruits should be turned once a day to ensure even drying.

When your apricots or tomatoes are wrinkled and dried, but not stiff, they are dehydrating, like a raisin. The texture becomes leathery, but malleable. If moisture beads remain on the fruit after it has been pulled open, they require extra sun exposure. Once they're done, keep them in airtight containers or sealed plastic bag to keep moisture out. No need to refrigerate.

Dough drying

In dough drying, the food is evaporated in a large container by exposure to heat. As soon as a dough-like, crumbly consistency is reached, the mass is spread out and dried with warm, dry air.

Solar Drying

In this process, the sun's rays are collected in a box that is specifically created for this purpose. This gives more about 30 degrees higher in temperature than when your dry food is in open sunlight. This makes the process faster, then but still not as efficient as with the use of a commercial dehydrator. In these first two processes, you need the weather to stay dry all throughout, or else, your food will absorb moisture and might spoil.

Vine Drying

This method is typically used to dry beans, such as kidney beans and navy beans. Leave the bean pods on the vine and allow nature to take its course. The beans can be picked when they are rattling inside. The process is also ideal for drying raisins.

Air Drying

Indoor air drying is possible if your home has adequate ventilation. This is a much gentler method of drying food, especially herbs. This process requires no action from us, but it takes a long time to dry because it relies on air to dry rather than heat.

The most important requirements are sufficient airflow, low humidity, and no direct sunlight. Air-drying is best done indoors, in a well-ventilated attic, room, or screened-in porch, or outdoors, behind a sun-protecting overhang. Herbs, mushrooms, and chili peppers are examples of air-dried foods.

Herbs are one of the simplest items to air-dry. If dried on a rack, herbs can be completely dry in two to three days. To save space, tie herbs into bundles and hang them from hooks or ceilings. This method can take two to three weeks to complete, but it has the added benefit of making the place smell wonderful in the meantime.

Curing, which is mostly done to onions and garlic after harvest, to help them store well, is a variation on air-drying. To do so, place onions or garlic in a warm, dry, well-ventilated location after harvestings, such as a shed or garage. Hang them from the rafters or spread them out in a single layer on a clean, dry area. The tops and necks should be completely dry after a few weeks, and the outer bulb peel should start to rustle. Before usage, remove the dry foliage above the bulbs and any roots.

FAQs About Using a Dehydrator

How long will dehydrated food last?

If prepared and stored properly, dehydrated food can last 5 to 10 years. But it is advisable to use your own within four to six months.

Does dehydrating food remove (or preserve) nutrients?

Yes, some nutrients are lost when food is dehydrated, but not significantly more than with other methods of preservation. The breakdown of vitamins is caused by heat and light. By extension, the canning method depletes more nutrients than the low heat, low moisture dehydrating method.

Blanching reduces the amount of thiamin and vitamin A and C that is lost from vegetables.

Does dehydrating food kill bacteria?

Provided that you dehydrate your vegetables and fruits until their moisture levels are anywhere between five and twenty percent, you have removed the bacteria that can cause food to decay. If you are concerned about bacteria on meat, it is recommended by the USDA that you first heat your raw meat to 160°F temperature and then dehydrate it at a steady temperature of 145°F.

Does Dehydrate Food Increase Sugar?

In most cases, yes, because dehydrating food at higher temperatures causes enzymes to die. More dense foods can withstand higher temperatures without losing enzymes. However, when the temperature rises between 140° and 160°F, most enzymes go dormant.

Can Cooked Food Be Dehydrated?

Yes. Meals can even be dehydrated, but some cooked food dehydrates better than others. If you are drying food for long-term storage, camping, or backpacking, you can prepare rice dishes, stews, and desserts and dry them by using nonstick sheets on the trays of a dehydrator. And then remove the nonstick sheet when they have reached a moist, crumbly consistency.

How can I store dried food?

If properly stored, dehydrated vegetables can last up to ten years and fruit up to five. The best way to store dried food for a long time is to vacuum seal it with an oxygen absorber and store it in a cool, dark place. Non-meat dried foods should be stored in reusable storage bags or freezer bags with the air squeezed out if they are to be consumed within 12 months.

If you plan to consume seafood and meat within a month, store them in freezer bags in a cool, dark place; otherwise, vacuum seal and freeze them. Meat can be kept in the freezer for up to a year if properly stored.

How to Store Herbs?

When completely dry, separate the leaves from the stems, and store the leaves (either whole or gently crumbled) in light-proof containers.

In terms of oven-drying, allow the dried herbs to cool and gently crush the leaves. Store the dried herbs in light-proof containers.

Store all your dried herbs in a cool dark place, in airtight containers.

Never store your herb vinegar in the sun or on a lighted counter if you intend to use them, no matter how pretty they look.

MEAT

Savory Chicken Jerky

Preparation Time: 12 hours | Dehydrating Time: 8 hours

Servings: 8

Ingredients

- 3 lb. chicken breasts
- 1 cup of Worcestershire sauce
- 1/4 cup of soy sauce
- 1 tsp garlic powder
- 1 tsp pepper

Directions

1. Chicken breasts should be sliced into long, thin strips that are less than an inch broad.
2. Mix all of the- ingredients in a large mixing bowl and marinate the chicken for at least an hour.
3. Place the chicken slices on your dehydrator, ensuring sure none of them contact.
4. Dehydrate for 8 hours at 160°F.

Salmon Jerky

Preparation Time 20 minutes | Dehydrating time: 5 hrs

Servings: 3

Ingredients

- 4 pounds salmon, cut in strips
- 1 cup of kosher salt
- 1 cup of brown sugar
- 1/2 cup of maple syrup or birch syrup

Directions

1. Mix the salt and sugar in a mixing bowl. Cover the bottom of a closed container with a thin coating of this. Arrange the salmon- strips in a single layer in the container. Cover with the last of the cure. If you need to do this in more than one layer, lightly sprinkle the first layer with the cure before adding the next layer of fish.

2. Refrigerate the container for 12 hours after covering it. Turn the jar upside down or stir the salmon pieces around once during this time to produce a more uniform curing.

3. Remove the salmon from the cure and swiftly submerge it in a big dish of cold water to remove any remaining cure. Dry the fish with paper -towels & place on a rack over a baking sheet in the refrigerator overnight if feasible, or for at least 1 hour in front of a fan or in a cool, shady, breezy location. The salmon's surface should become sticky-tacky, allowing smoke to attach to it.

4. Start your smoker. I aim for an interior temperature of around 200 degrees Fahrenheit. Your wood selections may be found in the headnotes. Smoke the salmon for at least 3 hours, or as long as it takes to dry out yet remain chewy. It usually takes me 5 hours to complete. If using maple syrup, brush it on the fish every 30 minutes or so after the first hour has passed.

5. Return the salmon jerky to the cooling rack to bring it back to room temperature. It will keep for -a long time at -room temperature (60F or lower), but I keep mine in tiny, vacuum-sealed packets in the fridge until I need it. It should persist for months in this condition.

Lamb With Rosemary Meatballs and Jerky

Preparation Time 20 minutes | Dehydrating time: 7 minutes

Servings: 3

Ingredients

- 1 pound ground lamb
- 2 cups of carrots
- 1 cup of spinach
- 1 cup of red onion diced
- 1 tbsp fresh rosemary chopped
- 1 tsp sea salt
- 1 tsp garlic powder
- 2 tsp ground turmeric
- 1 cup of dried apricots soaked (optional)
- 1/4 cup of date paste or medjool dates (optional)

Directions

1. Boil the carrots and onions until they are tender. Reduce carrots to 1 cup of if adding apricots and dates.
2. In a food processor, -mix the carrots, onions, spinach, rosemary, sea salt, garlic powder, and turmeric. If you're using the optional apricot and date paste, do so now.
3. Mix the ground lamb -with the vegetable mixture in a large mixing basin until thoroughly mixd.
4. Spread as thinly as possible onto jelly roll trays in the dehydrator. Depending on how thick it is, it will take 15-17 hours to dry. You may check halfway through and flip to finish drying. As it dries, you may split it up into smaller pieces.
5. Preheat your oven to 275 degrees, set the meat on a baking sheet, and flash heat for 10 minutes after drying it (especially ground beef).
6. Keep the container sealed. The apricot and date jerky will need

to be refrigerated.

7. If making meatballs for supper, use a 1/4 measuring cup of or a spoon to create big balls and bake at 375 degrees for 25 minutes. This recipe makes 12 to 13 big meatballs. Serve with spaghetti noodles cooked in the meatball juices or in a different oil of your choosing.

Ground Turkey Jerky

Preparation Time: 10 minutes | Dehydrating time: 10 hours

Servings: 1

INGREDIENTS

- 2 pounds of turkey flesh, ground
- Soy sauce, 1/3 cup
- Sauce Worcestershire (about a third of a cup) two or three dashes of Frank's hot sauce
- 1 tablespoon of maple syrup or honey
- a few freshly ground grinds of black pepper
- 2 teaspoons of powdered onion
- Red pepper flakes, 1 to 2 teaspoons (optional)

DIRECTIONS

1. Ground turkey meat should be placed halfway up a large zipper-seal bag. Normally, I double bag it to prevent spills from going everywhere.
2. In a large glass measuring cup, combine the remaining ingredients and mix them well.
3. Add the liquid mixture to the bag, then zip it up.
4. Jiggle, press, and poke the bag to make sure the liquid has completely covered the ground turkey flesh.

5. In the refrigerator, marinate for six hours to several days. I usually neglect mine for a few days!

6. You must line the dehydrator trays with parchment paper.

7. Half-fill the trays with the ground turkey mixture and press the meat into a thin layer with your palms.

8. It must be dried out for around ten hours at 140 degrees Fahrenheit. Your meat combination's thickness will determine whether it takes longer or less time.

9. The pans should be taken out of the oven, allowed to cool somewhat, and then cut into sticks using a pizza cutter.

10. For one month or up to six months, in the refrigerator, store or keep in an airtight container in a cold, dry location.

Thai Peanut Noodles with Chicken and Vegetables

Preparation time: 10 minutes | Dehydrating Time: 23 hours

Servings: 4

Ingredients:

- 1 cup pasta
- 1/4 cup chicken, chopped, dried and frozen
- 1/4 cup peanuts, roasted and chopped
- 1/4 cup mixed vegetables, dried and frozen
- 2 tablespoons peanut butter, powdered
- 1 1/2 teaspoon chicken flavor base, powdered
- 1 1/2 teaspoon cilantro, dried and frozen
- 1 teaspoon chia seeds
- 1/4 teaspoon garlic powder
- 1/4 teaspoon ginger, ground
- 1/4 teaspoon salt

- 1/8 teaspoon black pepper, ground
- Pinch of cayenne pepper, ground
- 1 cup water

Directions:

1. Dehydrate each ingredient that needs to be dried separately: chicken and mixed vegetables.
2. Follow required time and temperature for each.
3. Chicken – dry for 12 hours at 125 F Mixed vegetables – dry for 11 hours at 125 F
4. To Assemble:
5. Add all ingredients except the water in a resealable bag.
6. Store until ready to use.
7. To Rehydrate:
8. Bring water to a boil.
9. Rest the resealable bag on a bowl.
10. Open and pour in boiling water.
11. Seal. Soak for 9 minutes.
12. Turn upside down to mix.
13. Transfer to a bowl.

☆ ☆ ☆ ☆ ☆

Vietnamese jerky

Preparation time: 12 hours and 10 minutes. | Dehydration time: 6 hours | Servings: 4

Ingredients:

- 1 lb. Beef round
- Two tablespoons of fish sauce
- one tablespoon of soy sauce and two tablespoons of lime juice
- 1/4 cup brown sugar

Directions:

1. Combine all the ingredients in a bowl.
2. Transfer to a sealable plastic bag.
3. Turn to coat the beef strips evenly with the marinade.
4. Place in the refrigerator for 12 hours.
5. Drain the marinade.
6. Add the Beef to the color premium food dehydrator.
7. The process is at 165 degrees f for 6 hours.
8. Storage suggestions: store the jerky in a glass jar with a lid for up to 1 week.
9. Tip: slice the Beef across the grain. Make sure the Beef is at least 5 mm thick.

Chicken and Dumplings

Preparation time: 10 minutes | Dehydrating Time: 9 hours

Servings: 4

Ingredients:

- 1/4 cup dehydrated chicken
- 1 tablespoon dried peas
- 1 tablespoon dried carrots
- 1.5 teaspoon dried onion
- 1.5 teaspoon dried bell pepper
- 1 teaspoon dried chicken bouillon
- 1/2 teaspoon garlic powder
- 1/2 cup flour
- 1/2 tablespoon baking powder
- 2 tablespoons powdered milk
- 1/3 teaspoon dried dill
- 1/4 teaspoon salt

Directions:

1. In one bag, add chicken, vegetables, garlic, and soup base, plus salt and pepper to taste. (Remember, if your soup base or chicken bouillon isn't low sodium, you probably won't need extra salt!)
2. In a sandwich bag, add flour, baking powder, dried dill, salt, and milk.
3. To Rehydrate:
4. Add your bag of chicken and vegetables to a pot and top with 1 ½ cups of water. Turn your stove on and bring it to a boil.
5. Add ¼ cup of water to your powdered mix, seal, and use your fingers to 'mush' it around until all the liquid has been incorporated, and you're left with a wet, sticky dough.
6. Once your water comes to a boil, let cook for 2 minutes, stirring occasionally.
7. At the 2 minute mark, cut a slit in the corner of your dough bag, and squeeze small amounts of dumpling dough into the boiling liquid to create dumplings.
8. Boil for an additional minute after all your dumplings are in the liquid, then remove from heat, cover, and let sit for 5-8 minutes, or until your dumplings are cooked through.

☆ ☆ ☆ ☆ ☆

Teriyaki Beef Jerky

Preparation Time: 12 hours | Dehydrating time: 6 hours

Servings: 8 | Equipment: Dehydrator

Ingredients

- 2 lbs top round, sliced to 5-mm thick slices
- 1 Tbsp sesame oil
- 1/2 cup of soy sauce

- 1/4 cup of light brown sugar
- 1/4 tsp ginger, finely chopped
- 1 garlic clove, minced
- 1/4 cup of pineapple juice
- 1 Tbsp sesame seeds, optional

Directions

1. Cut the steak into 5-mm thick slices across the grain. Alternatively, have the meat sliced by the butcher.
2. In a large mixing bowl, mixd the sesame oil, soy sauce, light brown sugar, fresh garlic, pineapple juice, and sesame seeds.
3. Move the steak and marinade about in a gallon-size plastic bag until the meat is completely saturated.
4. Refrigerate for 12 to 24 hours after marinating.
5. The marinade should be drained and discarded.
6. Place the marinated meat on the dehydrator's wire trays. Expert Tip: You don't want to dry the marinade off the meat, but if the beef jerky sticks are dripping excessively, lightly pat any dripping liquid away.
7. Close the door and dehydrate for 6 hours at 165°F.
8. Serve right away, and keep the leftovers in an airtight container.

FRUITS

Apricot Fruit Leather

Preparation time: 15 minutes | Dehydrating time: 6-10 hours or more | Servings: 4

Ingredients:

- 4 cups Apricots, washed, pitted and sliced
- 1 Tbsp Lemon Juice
- 2-3 Tbsp Agave Nectar

Directions:

1. Add the ingredients into a saucepan and cook on medium-low for 20 minutes.
2. Allow to cool, transfer to your blender or food processor and pulse until smooth.
3. Line your dehydrator trays with parchment paper or fruit leather sheets, grease them and spread the puree into ¼-inch layers.
4. Dehydrate at 130F / 54C for 6-10 hours or until dry to the touch.
5. Place on parchment paper, slice into strips, roll up and store in airtight containers.

Banana Cocoa Leather

Preparation time: 15 minutes | Dehydrating time: 15 hours

Servings: 4

Ingredients:

- 4 bananas
- 2 Tbsp cocoa powder
- 1-2 Tbsp corn syrup

- 1 tsp. lemon juice

Directions:

1. Puree all ingredients until smooth.

2. Pour mixture onto dehydrator trays and spread to ¼ inch thickness. Dehydrate at 130 degree for 8-10 hours. About half way through, flip leather to the other side.

Cherry Coconut Almond Cookies

Preparation time: 20 minutes | Dehydrating time: 6 hours

Servings: 4

Ingredients:

- 1 cup salted almond butter
- 1 cup pitted dates (soaked in water for 1/2 hour)
- 1 cup dried cherries (soaked in water for 1/2 hour)
- 1 cup crushed almonds
- 1/8-1/4 cup water
- 1 cup shredded coconut

Directions:

1. In a food processor, pulse the dried fruits. Add almond butter and crushed almonds. Pulse again.

2. Add in water slowly until the dough is able to be rolled into balls. Do not allow dough to get too runny. Flatten balls into discs and dip into shredded coconut to adhere to both sides.

3. Place on dehydrator sheet and set temperature to 145 degrees. Dehydrate for 3 hours and then flip over to other side for 3 hours.

Dehydrated Blueberries

Preparation time: 15 minutes | Dehydrating time: 8 hrs

Servings: 4

Ingredients:

- frozen or fresh blueberries

Directions

1. Wash and remove any undesirable fruit from fresh blueberries.
2. By placing blueberries in a mesh strainer, submerging them for 30 seconds in boiling water, and then shocking them with cold water to halt the cooking, blueberries can be chopped, punctured, or "checked." The skin becomes more permeable as a result, enabling moisture from within to escape.
3. Punctured or examined blueberries should be placed on mesh trays with some room between each berry. Dry at 135°F (57°C) for 8-18 hours. Dehydrator, berry size, house temperature, and humidity affect drying time. Food dehydrates rapidly in my prairie home in the winter.
4. Rotate the pans after six hours and check the blueberries to see how quickly they are drying.
5. The completed blueberries will be supple and leathery with no signs of moisture when pressed or cut open. Blueberries may become a little bit sticky due to their natural sugar content. At first, it's challenging to distinguish between damp and sticky, but you'll get the hang of it. If you're unsure, dry the berries for a little while longer or let them cool. As they cool, they will become more rigid. On the tray, let it cool for at least two hours.
6. The place once completely cooled in an airtight container (a glass jar is best). For the following seven days, keep an eye on and shake the container to condition the blueberries and make

sure they are absolutely dry. If the blueberries soften and group together, or if you see any moisture on the jar's edges, put them back in the dehydrator. Put it somewhere cold and dark for a year if everything seems well.

☆ ☆ ☆ ☆ ☆

Dehydrated Cherries

Preparation Time: 10 minutes | Dehydrating time: 8 hours

Servings: 4

Ingredients

- Lemon juice washed
- 2 pounds of destemmed pitted cherries (optional topping)

Directions

1. It is necessary to wash, destem, and pit the cherries. Place whole or sliced cherries on the trays (see notes). They look more like dried cherries from the store when I slice them in half. Cherries should be added to the dehydrator rack until the top level is full. Fill each tier to the brim, leaving room between each cherry to allow for air circulation. Lemon juice is optional but may be drizzled on top if preferred.

2. With the cover closed, preheat the dehydrator to 135°F. It will take the cherries anything between 6 and 10 hours to thoroughly dehydrate. After six hours, start examining them. The ideal state is somewhat rubbery but not wet. After cooling, they will get stiffer.

☆ ☆ ☆ ☆ ☆

Dehydrating Nectarine

Preparation Time: 20 minutes | Dehydrating time: 8 hours

Servings: 4

Ingredients:

- 10 nectarines or peveryes

Directions

1. After being separated and the stone removed to promote consistent drying, it is quite simple to dry everything in a dehydrator.
2. To prepare everything, use a sulfite solution, an acid solution, or sugar blanching. There are specific Directions for each, which may be found above.
3. On the dehydrator racks, arrange the fruit in a way that leaves adequate room for even airflow.
4. After that, the dehydrator's racks may be placed inside to start the drying process.
5. In a dehydrator set at around 50C/120F, each will require 6–10 hours to dehydrate.

VEGETABLES

Candied pumpkin

Preparation Time: 15 minutes | Dehydrating time: 8 hours

Servings: 2

Ingredients:

- 1 cup coconut milk
- 2 cups applesauce
- 2 cups pumpkin puree
- 1/4 cup honey
- 1/2 teaspoon ground allspice
- 1/2 teaspoon ground nutmeg
- 1 teaspoon ground cinnamon
- 1/4 cup coconut flakes
- 2 tablespoons dried cranberries, chopped

Directions:

1. Combine all the ingredients in a bowl.
2. Spread the mixture in the fruit leather sheet of your cosori premium food dehydrator.
3. Dehydrate at 135 degrees f for 8 hours.
4. Storage suggestions: slice the fruit leather before storing in a food container with lid.

Tip:

grease the fruit leather sheet with a little bit of oil before processing.

☆ ☆ ☆ ☆ ☆

Dehydrated Sweet Peppers

Preparation & Dehydrating time: 12 hours and 10 minutes

Servings: 5

Ingredients:

- 4 cups bell peppers, sliced into strips

Directions

1. Add the bell pepper strips to the dehydrator.
2. Dehydrate at 135 degrees F for 12 hours.

Dehydrated Celery

Preparation & Dehydrating time: 15 hours and 5 minutes

Servings: 5

Ingredients:

- 4 cups celery, sliced

Directions

1. Add the celery slices to your dehydrator.
2. Dehydrate at 125 degrees F for 15 hours.
3. Store in an airtight container.

Dehydrated Raw Vegan Oat and Buckwheat Crunch with Flaxseed

Preparation Time: 30 minutes |Dehydrating Time: 10 hours

Servings: 4

Ingredients

- Soaking overnight (optional)
- 7 1/3 oz Buckwheat
- 1 oz of Medjool Dates (large dates)
- 45 ml Tap water (mineral water, drinking) (1.6 oz)
- 1 tsp ground cinnamon (0.09 oz)
- 7 1/3 oz Rolled oats (raw?)
- 1 3/4 oz Flaxseed (Linseed), raw (organic?)

Directions:

1. In a blender, combine the dates, water, and cinnamon to make a date paste. If required, add water to get a paste-like consistency.
2. Make raw rolled oats from oat groats or purchase raw rolled oats
3. The original recipe calls for 100 g dates and 125 mL water for 10 servings. These figures have been purposefully reduced
4. Toss the buckwheat with the date paste, then add the flaxseed and rolled oats. All of the components should be thoroughly combined. If the mixture appears to be dry, add a little more water.
5. Divide the mixture evenly across two dehydrator trays. Dehydrate for 12-15 hours at 42°C, or until completely dry.

Summery Eggplant Jerky

Preparation Time:1 hour |Dehydrating time: 6 hours

Servings: 4

Ingredients

- 1 Eggplant
- 8 oz Eggplant (Evenly Sliced)

Marinade

- 1/4 Cup of Balsamic
- 1 tsp Avocado oil
- 1/2 tsp Garlic powder
- 1/4 tsp Parsley
- 1/4 tsp Pink Salt
- 1/2 tsp Oregano
- 1/2 tsp Red Pepper Flakes
- 3/4 Cup of Vegetable Broth

Directions:

1. Cut the eggplant into even slices.
2. To remove the bitterness from the eggplant slices, soak them in a dish of salted water for 40 minutes.
3. Strain the eggplant slices through a sieve and place them on a paper towel to dry.
4. To prepare the marinade, whisk together all of the ingredients.
5. Marinate the eggplant slices in a ziplock bag with the marinade for 4 to 12 hours in the refrigerator.
6. After marinating, drain in a colander.
7. Place the eggplant strips on a paper towel and gently dry them to remove any excess moisture.
8. Place eggplant slices on dehydrator trays.
9. In a dehydrator, dehydrate for 4 to 6 hours at 145 degrees Fahrenheit.

10. Check the texture after 4 hours and continue to dry to your satisfaction.

Cinnamon Carrots

Preparation time: 10 minutes | Dehydrating time: 10 hours

Servings: 4

Ingredients

- 10 oz shredded carrots
- 3/4 tsp ground cinnamon
- 1 tbsp granulated sugar
- 2 tbsp coconut oil, melted
- 1/2 tsp sea salt

Directions:

1. Add melted coconut oil in a large bowl. Add sugar, cinnamon, and salt to the bowl and stir well.
2. Add shredded carrots to the bowl and toss well to coat.
3. Arrange shredded carrots on dehydrator trays and dehydrate at 125 F/ 52 C for 8-10 hours.

Nutrition:

Calories: 100; Total Fat: 6.8g; Saturated Fat: 5.9g; Protein: 0.6g; Carbs: 10.3g; Fiber:

Dried sweet Potatos

Preparation Time: 10 minutes | Dehydrating time: 12 hours

Servings: 4

Ingredients:

- 2 sweet potatoes
- 1 teaspoon onion powder

Directions:

1. Season the sweet potato slices with onion powder.
2. Arrange in a single layer in the cosori premium food dehydrator.
3. Set at 115 degrees f.
4. Process for 12 hours.

Storage suggestions: Store in a sealable plastic bag.

Tip: use a mandolin slicer to prepare the sweet potatoes.

☆ ☆ ☆ ☆ ☆

HERBS AND POWDERS

Dried herb mix

Preparation Time: 15 minutes | Dehydrating time: 8 hours

Serving: 5

Ingredients:

- 1/2 cup thyme leaves
- 1/2 cup rosemary leaves
- 2 teaspoons lemon zest
- 6 cloves garlic, peeled

Directions:

1. Combine all the ingredients in a food processor.
2. Pulse until smooth.
3. Spread the mixture in the cosori premium food dehydrator.
4. Dehydrate at 135 degrees f for 8 hours.

Storage suggestions: store in an empty spice bottle.

Tip: you can also add other herbs into the mix such as oregano or thyme.

Dehydrate Lettuce and Make Lettuce Powder

Preparation Time: 5 minutes | Dehydrating time: 8 hrs

Servings: 7

Ingredients

- Any type of lettuce

Directions

1. Wash Place on dehydrator trays; loosely packed is preferred, but because they shrink rapidly, it's okay to pack a bit. Dry at 95°F (35°C) for 6–10 hours or at 125°F (52°C) for 4–6 hours.

Onion powder

Preparation Time: 10 minutes | Dehydrating time: 8 hours

Serving: 5

Ingredients:

- 5 onions, sliced

Directions:

1. Arrange the onion slices in a single layer in the cosori premium food dehydrator.
2. Dehydrate at 145 degrees f for 8 hours.
3. Transfer the dried onion to a food processor.
4. Pulse until powdery.

Storage suggestions: store the onion powder in a mason jar.

Leek powder

Preparation Time: 5 minutes | Dehydrating time: 12 hours

Serving: 5

Ingredients:

- 4 cups leeks, sliced

Directions:

1. Place the leeks in the cosori premium food dehydrator.
2. Dehydrate at 135 degrees f for 4 hours.
3. Put the dried leeks in a spice grinder.
4. Grind until powdery.

Storage suggestions: store in a tightly sealed food or spice container.

Tip: do not use any browned parts of leeks.

Dried parsley, basil & oregano powder

Preparation Time: 15 minutes | Dehydrating time: 8 hours

Servings: 5

Ingredients:

- 2 tablespoons parsley leaves
- 2 tablespoons basil leaves
- 2 tablespoons oregano leaves
- 2 tablespoons brown sugar
- 2 tablespoons salt

Directions:

1. Add the herb leaves to the cosori premium food dehydrator.
2. Dehydrate at 135 degrees f for 8 hours.
3. Transfer the dried leaves to a food processor.
4. Stir in the sugar and salt.

Storage suggestions: store in a mason jar with lid.

Tip: you can also skip the sugar and salt, and simply mix the dried herbs.

Dried Lemon, Thyme, Garlic & Rosemary Mix

Preparation & Dehydrating time: 20 hours and 15 minutes

Servings: 2

Ingredients:

- 2 teaspoons lemon zest

- 1/2 cup fresh thyme leaves
- 1/2 cup fresh rosemary leaves
- 8 garlic cloves, peeled

Directions:

1. Add the lemon zest, thyme leaves, rosemary leaves and garlic cloves to a food processor.
2. Pulse until fully chopped.
3. Spread the mixture on the dehydrator tray.
4. Dehydrate at 130 degrees F for 20 hours.
5. Store in an airtight container.

Rosemary, Thyme, Lemon and Garlic Dried Herb Mix

Preparation & Dehydrating time: 10 hours and 30 minutes

Servings: 2

Ingredients

- rosemary stalks removed, 1/4 cup
- removed 3/4 cup of the thyme stalks
- Removed oregano stems from 1/2 cup zested
- 3 medium lemons
- 3 tablespoons of dried garlic flakes
- 1 tbsp. Sea salt (optional)

Directions

1. Heat the oven to 120–170°F with a rack in the center.
2. Herbs and lemon zest should be roasted in the oven's center. Stir the herbs every 30 minutes for 2-4 hours in the oven.
3. When the herb mixture is dry, remove it from the oven. Cool

herbs. Once cool ed and dry, transfer the mixture to a basin. Combine herbs, salt, and garlic with your fingers. Put the mixture in an airtight jar.

Mushroom Powder

Preparation Time: 15 minutes | Dehydration Time: 12 hours

Servings: 15

Ingredients:

- 2 cups shiitake mushrooms

Directions:

1. Arrange the shiitake mushrooms in a single layer in the Cosori Premium Food Dehydrator.
2. Dry at 135 degrees F for 12 hours.
3. Place the dried mushrooms in a food processor.
4. Pulse until powdered.
5. Storage Suggestions: Store in a glass jar with lid. Place the jar in an area with low light.
6. Preparation & Dehydration Tips: You can also make this recipe using other types of mushrooms.

Porcini Cubes

Preparation Time: 20 minutes | Dehydration Time: 10 hours

Servings: 15

Ingredients:

- 2 oz. dried porcini mushrooms

- 2 teaspoons gelatin powder
- 3 tablespoons onion powder
- 2 tablespoons soy sauce
- 1 teaspoon fish sauce
- 1 tablespoon water
- 2 teaspoons salt

Directions:

1. Combine all the ingredients in a bowl.
2. Form small balls from the mixture.
3. Shape into cubes.
4. Add the cubes to the Cosori Premium Food Dehydrator.
5. Dry at 125 degrees F for 10 hours.

Storage Suggestions: Wrap the cubes in foil and store in a cool dry place for up to 1 week.

Preparation & Dehydration Tips: Homemade onion powder gives the best results for this recipe.

CRACKERS

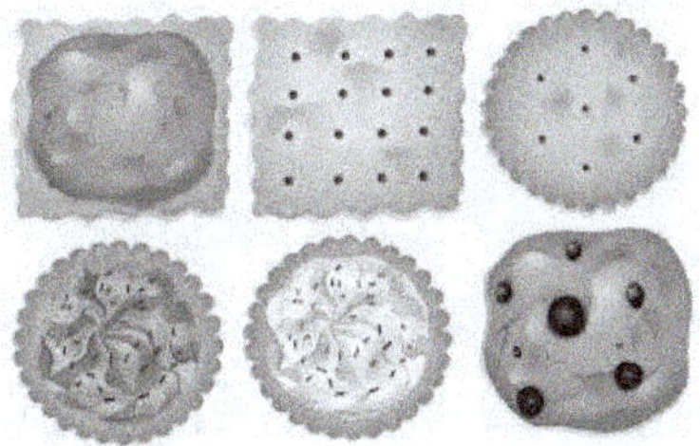

Herb and almond crackers

Preparation Time: 10 minutes | Dehydrating time: 12 hours

Servings: 4

Ingredients:

- 2 cups almonds
- 1/2 cup ground flax seeds
- 1/4 cup brewer's yeast
- 3/4 cups water
- 2 tablespoons fresh rosemary, finely chopped
- 1 teaspoon salt
- 1/2 teaspoon black pepper

Directions:

1. In a food processor, combine the almonds, flax seed, yeast, salt, and pepper. Pulse until well combined.
2. Slowly add the water while continuing to pulse until a paste forms.
3. Place paraflexx screens on the racks of your excalibur and spread a thin layer of the paste onto each screen. Set your excalibur to 115f and dehydrate for 12 hours or until the crackers are crispy. Remove from the screens and break into small pieces to serve.

Carrot crackers

Preparation Time: 20 minutes | Dehydrating time: 12 hours

Servings: 12

Ingredients:

- 6 large carrots, peeled

- 1/2 cup ground flax seeds
- 1 tomato, diced
- Juice from 1 lemon
- 1/2 cup sesame seeds
- 1/2 cup chia seeds
- 3/4 cups water

Directions:

1. In a food processor, combine the carrots, flax seeds, tomato, lemon juice, and water, and pulse until a paste forms. Add the chia seeds and sesame seeds and stir to combine.
2. Place paraflexx screens on the racks of your excalibur food dehydrator. Spread the paste evenly on the screens about 1/4 inch thick.
3. Set your excalibur to 105f and dehydrate for 12 hours. Remove the crackers from the excalibur and allow cooling completely. The crackers will become crispy as they cool.

Mexican crackers

Preparation Time: 30 minutes | Dehydrating time: 6 hours

Servings: 15

Ingredients:

- 1/2 cup chia seeds
- 1 cup golden flaxseeds
- 1/2 cup pumpkin seeds
- 1/2 cup sunflower seeds
- 1 red bell pepper, chopped
- 1/4 onion, chopped
- 1 cup carrot pulp
- 1 1/2 teaspoons chipotle powder

- 1 teaspoon garlic powder
- Salt to taste
- 1/2 teaspoon cayenne pepper

Directions:

1. In a blender process all the seeds until powdery.
2. Stir in the bell pepper and onion.
3. Pulse until smooth.
4. Stir in the rest of the ingredients.
5. Pulse until fully combined.
6. Spread the mixture in the cosori premium food dehydrator.
7. Score the crackers.
8. Dry at 115 degrees f for 6 hours.

Storage suggestions: store in a sealed food container for up to 5 days.

Tip: soak the seeds in separate bowls of water for 6 hours before processing.

Raw Crackers

Preparation time: 20 Minutes | Dehydrating time: 15 Hours

Servings: 4

Ingredients:

For the crackers:

- 3 cups organic carrot pulp
- 3/4 cup filtered/purified water
- 1/2 cup organic ground flax seeds
- 1 organic tomato
- 1 tablespoon organic lemon juice

For the add-ins:

- 1/2 cup organic chia seeds

- 1/2 cup organic sesame seeds

Directions

1. **Please Note:** This recipe requires 10-12 dehydrating time.
2. Add all the ingredients for the crackers in a blender and blend until everything is well combined and the mixture has a thick paste-type consistency.
3. After you've made the cracker mixture, transfer the cracker mixture to a medium-size bowl and add the chia seed + sesame seed add-ins, then stir them into the cracker mixture.
4. Spread the cracker mixture evenly onto the non-stick dehydrator sheets of a dehydrator tray, taking care to not spread it too thick or too thin.
5. Dehydrate at 105 F for approximately 8-12 hours (I suggest doing this overnight)
6. Remove the crackers from the sheet and transfer them to a mesh dehydrator tray and dehydrate for an additional 2-6 hours, or until they are hard and crisp.
7. Cut into small bite-size cracker pieces and store in an air-tight container.

Store: Now we already know that the dehydrator will remove all the moisture from the crackers so it's very important that you properly store the crackers to keep them crisp. Make sure you store them in an air-tight container until ready to serve. Even the air has moisture in it so leaving them out in the open will cause them to get soft. I advise to use glass storage containers for dehydrated items, as well as for other food storage.

Hazelnut Lemon Crackers

Preparation time: 15 minutes | Dehydrating time: 7 hours

Servings: 4

Ingredients:

- 1/2 cup chia seeds
- 1 cup water
- 3 cups hazelnuts, soaked overnight, skins removed
- 1 1/2 tbsp. Lemon zest
- 1 tbsp. Maple syrup
- 1/2 tsp. Sea salt
- Black pepper to taste

Directions:

1. Mix chia seeds in 1 cup of water then let soften.
2. Remove soaked hazelnuts then drain them. Place hazelnuts in a food processor then grind until fine.
3. Pour ground nuts into a bowl then combine with chia seeds, lemon zest, maple syrup, salt and pepper.
4. Spread onto dehydrator trays. Use a spatula to flatten the dough to approximately 1/4 inch thick. Dehydrate at 145 degrees for 1 hour. Decrease the heat to 115 and continue to dehydrate for 8 hours.

Macadamia-Sage Crackers

Preparation time: 15 minutes | Dehydrating time: 6 hours

Servings: 4

Ingredients:

- 2 cups macadamia nuts

- 2 cups chia or flax seeds
- 1 1/2 tbsp. Fresh sage, crushed
- Sea salt and white pepper to taste
- 3 cups water
- 1/2 cup olive oil

Directions:

1. Put macadamia nuts and flax seeds into a food processor then grind into flour. Add sage, salt and pepper. Process until you have a fine texture.
2. Add water to nut and seed mix in a huge bowl, then stir until thick. Don't pour all the water at once. Add little amounts until a soft dough forms.
3. Spread onto dehydrator sheets. Sprinkle with olive oil then sprinkle additional sea salt.
4. Dehydrate at 110 deg. F for 4 hrs. Score the crackers, flip them over then dehydrate another 8 hours.

Bagel Flax Crackers

Preparation Time: 5 minutes | Dehydrating Time: 24 hours

Servings: 24

Ingredients:

- 3 tsp of sea salt
- 3 tsp of onion flakes
- 3 tsp of garlic flakes
- 3 tsp of sesame seeds
- 3 tsp of poppy seeds
- 1 clove garlic
- 1 1/2 cups of water
- 3/4 cup of golden flax seeds

- 1/4 cup of brown flax seeds

Directions:

1. Combine the water and garlic in a food processor, blender, or Nutribullet. Pour over flax seeds. Soak for around 3 and a half hours. The mixture will eventually turn gelatinous.
2. Spread the mixture onto a Teflon sheet to a thickness of ⅛ and ¼ inch. Make squares out of the mix using a knife to cut lines into the crackers to create grids.
3. Combine the spices in a bowl, excluding the table salt. It would be best if you sprinkled everything mixed on top of the crackers. After that, sprinkle some coarse sea salt on top.
4. Dehydrate at 110°F for 24 hours or until the food is crispy.

CHIPS

Beet Chips

Preparation time: 20 minutes | Dehydrating time: 4 hours in the dehydrator. | Servings: 6

Ingredients:

- 1⁄2-pound fresh beetroots

Directions:

1. Slice the prepared beets paper-thin with a mandolin.
2. Lay the sliced beets out onto dehydrator trays.
3. Set the dehydrator to 125 F and dry the chips for approximately 3 to 4 hours. (Drying time could varies depending on the thickness of the chips and the humidity level near your dehydrator)
4. Serve or store in an airtight container. Depending on how dried out the chips are, they are probably good for at least few weeks. They are easily squashed if stored in a bag, so opt for a sturdier container.

Applications:

1. Add a handful of dried beets to your next red berry smoothie. The color of the beets will improve the color of your drink, and the sweetness of the beets will enhance the strawberry, cherry, or raspberry flavor.
2. Make a quick, cold beet soup. Mix the dried beets in a blender or food processor with plain yogurt or sour cream. Dilute with milk to the desired thickness and season with salt and pepper.
3. Serve with extra dried beets and dried dill as a garnish.

Zucchini chips

Preparation Time: 15 minutes | Dehydrating time: 12 hours

Servings: 8

Ingredients:

- 4 cups zucchini, sliced thinly
- 2 tbsp. Balsamic vinegar
- 2 tbsp. Olive oil
- 2 tsp. Sea salt

Directions:

1. Add olive oil, balsamic vinegar, and sea salt to the large bowl and stir well.
2. Add sliced zucchini to the bowl and toss well.
3. Arrange zucchini slices on dehydrator trays and dehydrate at 135 f/ 58 c for 8-12 hours.
4. Store in air-tight container.

Brussels sprout chips

Preparation Time: 15 minutes | Dehydrating time: 6 hours

Servings: 4

Ingredients:

- 2 lbs. Brussels sprouts, wash, dry, cut the root and separate leaves
- 2 fresh lemon juice
- 1/2 cup water
- 1/4 cup nutritional yeast
- 1 jalapeno pepper halved and remove seeds
- 1 cup cashews

- 2 bell peppers
- 1 tsp. Sea salt

Directions:

1. Add brussels sprouts leaves to the large bowl and set aside.
2. Add bell peppers, water, lemon juice, nutritional yeast, jalapeno, cashews, and salt to the blender and blend until smooth.
3. Pour blended mixture over brussels sprouts leaves and toss until well coated.
4. Arrange brussels sprouts on dehydrator trays and dehydrate at 125 f/ 52 c for 6 hours.
5. Allow to cool completely then store in air-tight container.

Dehydrator Chivy Cheese Chips

Preparation Time: 5 minutes

Dehydrating time: 4 hours

Servings: 4

Ingredients:

- 1 (12 ounces) carton cottage cheese with chives
- 1 medium cut of ripe tomatoes in quarters
- 1 tbsp chopped onion
- 1 dash cayenne
- 1 dash of garlic powder

Directions

1. Blend cottage cheese, tomato, onion, and seasonings till smooth in a blender or food processor.
2. Spoon 1 1/2 to 2" diameter spoonfuls of mixture onto fruit roll sheets.

3. Dry for 4 to 6 hours at 145 degrees Fahrenheit, or until the rounds curl up on the edges like potato chips.

Apple Rings and Apple Chips

Preparation time: 5minutes | Dehydrating time: 5 hours

Servings: 6

Ingredients:

- Apples
- Cinnamon (optional)
- Lemon juice (optional)

Directions:

1. Peel, core, and cut the apples into slices about 1/4 inch thick, making use of apple peeler, apple corer, and apple slicer.

2. Follow my directions on options to dip your fruits in preservative water to prevent them from browning if desired.

3. Arrange your apple slices on the dehydrator trays, making sure they do not overlap. Next, sprinkle them with lemon juice and cinnamon mixture, optional.

4. Dehydrate at 135 degrees F temperature for ten to twelve hours, until apple rings are leathery but not crispy. If you prefer dehydrated apples that are more like apple chips, give them more time to dehydrate. Let cool completely before storing.

5. To store for several months, transfer your dried apples into vacuum seal bags and vacuum seal. Or store for a few months in an airtight container or zip-lock bags. For best longevity, store in a cool, dark place.

Pumpkin Chips

Preparation Time: 15 minutes | Dehydrating time: 18 hours 10 minutes | Servings: 6

Ingredients:

- 1 pumpkin
- 2 tablespoons coconut oil, melted
- 1 teaspoon cinnamon
- 1 teaspoon nutmeg

Directions:

1. Remove the seeds, pulp, and skin from the pumpkin, and slice the pumpkin flesh into thin slices.
2. Try to make the slices no more than 1/8 inch thick.
3. In a large bowl, combine the pumpkin slices, coconut oil, cinnamon, nutmeg, and salt. Stir well to coat.
4. Place the pumpkin slices on the racks of your Excalibur and set to 125F. Dehydrated for 18 hours or until the slices are crispy.

Eggplant Chips

Preparation Time: 30 minutes | Dehydrating time: 6 hours 15 minutes | Servings: 6

Ingredients:

- 4 baby eggplants, sliced thin
- 3 tablespoons olive oil
- 1/2 teaspoon smoked paprika
- 1/2 teaspoon oregano
- 1/4 teaspoon cayenne pepper

- 2 tablespoons salt

Directions:

1. In a large bowl, combine the eggplant slices olive oil, paprika, oregano, cayenne pepper, and salt.
2. Place the eggplant slices on the racks of your Excalibur and set to 135F.
3. Dehydrate for 5 to 6 hours or until eggplant slices are entirely dried and crispy.

SNACKS

Sunflower seeds

Preparation Time: 13 minutes | Dehydrating Time: 16 hours

Servings: 4

Ingredients:

- 3 cup uncooked shelled sunflower seeds
- 2 tablespoons olive oil
- 1 tablespoon onion powder
- 1 tablespoon celery salt
- 1 tablespoon soy sauce
- 1 tablespoon garlic powder
- 1/2 tablespoon crushed red pepper flakes

Directions:

1. Soak sunflower seeds overnight in a bowl. Rinse and pat dry.
2. Combine the seeds with the remaining

Ingredients:

Place on a dehydrator pan and dehydrate for 16 hours at 115°F.

Savory crisps

Preparation time: 15 minutes | Dehydration time: 6 hours

Servings: 4

Ingredients:

- One Vidalia onion, peeled and halved
- Two cloves of garlic, peeled and ground
- 1 cup of ground flax seeds
- 1 cup ground chia seeds
- 1 1/2 cups ground sunflower seeds

- 1/2 cup low-sodium soy sauce
- 1/2 cup extra virgin olive oil
- 1/2 tsp. White pepper

Directions:

1. Process onions and garlic, but don't make a paste.
2. Mix the remaining ingredients. Combine.
3. Spread the mixture on a dehydrator sheet and dehydrate at 100 degrees for 24-36 hours.
4. After dehydrating, cut into large squares.

Sweet and salty pumpkin seeds

Preparation time: 15 minutes | Dehydration time: 6 hours

Servings: 4

Ingredients:

- 2 cups pumpkin seeds
- 2 tbsp. Olive oil
- 1 tbsp. Paprika
- 1 tbsp. Turmeric
- 1 tbsp. Sugar
- 1 tsp. Ground ginger

Directions:

1. Soak pumpkin seeds in enough water to cover them for a full night. Dry the seeds and mix everything else. Mix the seeds until they are completely covered. Put on a tray for the dehydrator. Dehydrate at 105 to 115 degrees for 12 to 18 hours.

☆ ☆ ☆ ☆ ☆

Sundried tomato flax crackers

Preparation time: 15 minutes | Dehydration time: 6 hours

Servings: 4

Ingredients:

- 1 cup flax seeds
- 1 cup water
- 1 tbsp. Dried basil
- 1/2 tbsp. Dried thyme
- 2 tbsp. Sundried tomatoes, ground
- 1 tbsp. Extra-virgin olive oil
- 1 tsp. Flaky sea salt

Directions:

1. All ingredients, except for the salt, should be mixed in a large bowl until they stick together. It should take about an hour to do this. Spread the mixture on the dehydrator sheets so it's about 1/8 to 1/4 inch thick. Add a little sea salt. Dehydrate for 4 hours with a temperature of 105 degrees.
2. Turn the mixture over and score it. Keep losing water for another 6–6 hours.

Savory trail mix

Preparation time: 15 minutes | Dehydration time: 6 hours

Servings: 4

Ingredients:

- 1 cup raw almonds, soaked and dried
- 1 cup raw pumpkin seeds, washed and dried

- 1 cup raw sunflower seeds, soaked and dried
- 3 tbsp. Low sodium soy sauce
- 3 tbsp. Olive oil
- 1 tsp. Garlic powder
- 2 tsp. Onion powder
- 1/2 tsp. Celery salt
- Pinch of cayenne pepper

Directions:

1. Combine the soy sauce, olive oil, and seasonings in a mixing bowl. Pour over nuts and seeds and toss until evenly covered.
2. Using mesh sheets, spread the mixture onto the dehydrator tray.
3. Dehydrate for 18 hours at 105-115 degrees Fahrenheit.

Seasoned seeds

Preparation time: 15 minutes. | Dehydration time: 6 hours

Servings: 4

Ingredients:

- 1 Tbsp. Olive oil
- 1 tbsp. Soy sauce
- 1/2 tsp. Garlic powder
- 1/2 tsp. Onion powder
- 1/2 tsp. Celery salt
- 1/4 tsp. Crushed red pepper flakes
- Two cups of shelled sunflower seeds, raw

Directions:

1. Soak sunflower seeds overnight. Thoroughly rinse and dry.
2. Combine the olive oil, soy sauce, and seasonings in a mixing

bowl. Toss the seeds in the mixture until evenly coated.

3. Dehydrate on a dehydrator tray for 12-18 hours at 105-115 degrees.

SWEETS AND DESSERTS

Very spicy gingerbread cookies

Preparation Time: 5 minutes | Dehydrating Time: 10 hours

Servings: 4

Ingredients:

- 2 1/4 cups all-purpose flour
- 2 teaspoons of baking soda
- 1 teaspoon ground cinnamon
- 3/4 cup (1 1/2 sticks) butter, softened
- 1 1/4 cups more 1/3 cup sugar
- 1/2 cup of molasses
- 1 large egg
- 1 tablespoon coarse ground dry ginger

Directions:

1. Preheat oven to 350 ° F. Sprays a large baking sheet with cooking spray.
2. In a medium bowl, combine flour, baking powder, and cinnamon.
3. In a large bowl, beat butter and 1¼ cups sugar until creamy. Add the molasses, egg, and ginger and beat until smooth. Add flour mixture in three additions, mixing well after each.
4. Roll the dough into 1-inch balls and roll the remaining ⅓ cup of sugar to coat. Place 2 inches apart on the baking sheet. Press them with the palm of your hand to make a thick disc. Bake until edges are lightly browned, 10 to 12 minutes. Chill on the baking sheet for 5 minutes, then remove to a wire rack to cool completely. Store in an airtight container.

Walnut and Apricot Cookies

Preparation time: 20 Minutes | Dehydrating time: 10 Hours

Servings: 4

Ingredients:

- Overnight soaked Walnuts 2 cups
- Sweet and sour fresh apricots or dried 1 cup
- Soaked Raisins 1 small cup
- Over-ripe bananas 2

Directions:

1. Use a blender to blend the batter to the crumby consistency and spoon out on any dehydrator tray.
2. Dehydrate at a temperature of 105 F for 24 hours, or until dry (do not over dehydrate).
3. Switch them over within 8-12 hours, or when one portion is dry enough.
4. Experiment with the nuts, beans, and fruits you want. A mix of fresh fruit and a few dried, soaked fruits with nuts is also nice. You can use sunflower seeds for veggie/'salty crackers, and they appear to offer a salty taste when dry. You can, of course, include some other soaked nuts/seeds.

Chewy Soft Lemon Cookies

Preparation Time: 20 minutes | Dehydrating time: 50 minutes

Servings: 4

Ingredients:

- 2 cups of + 2 TB all purpose flour

- 1 TB cornstarch
- 1/2 tsp baking soda
- 1/2 tsp table salt
- 3/4 cup of salted butter, softened to room temp but not melty
- 1 1/4 cups of granulated (white) sugar
- zest of 2 whole lemons
- 1 large egg
- 1 large egg olk
- 2 TB freshly squeezed lemon juice
- 1 1/2 tsp vanilla extract

For the Lemon Icing:

- 1 cup of powdered sugar
- 2 TB fresh lemon juice
- 1 TB fresh lemon zest

Directions

1. Preheat the oven- at 350 degrees F and place the rack in the lower middle position.
2. Whisk together the flour, -cornstarch, baking soda, and salt in a mixing basin until well mixd. Set aside.
3. Using the paddle attachment, -mix the butter, sugar, and zest in the bowl of a stand mixer on medium high speed. Approximately 3 mins, or until light and fluffy. Blend in the egg and egg yolk just until mixd. Mix the lemon juice and vanilla essence in a mixing bowl. Blend until well mixd.
4. Fold the dry ingredients into the wet components using a rubber spatula. Fold together until there are no dry lumps left and the dough forms a single large ball.
5. Wrap the dough in plastic- wrap & refrigerate for 1 hour or more. (The dough can be refrigerated- for a day or two at this stage before using.)
6. Preheat oven to 350°F. Line baking pans with parchment

paper. Form 1 inch round dough balls and arrange 2 inches apart on parchment paper. Bake for 8-9 mins, or til the cookie is puffy and brown. It will appear somewhat underdone at first, but they will firm up as they cool. Don't overcook the potatoes.

7. Allow cookies to cool completely on baking pans before transferring to wire rack.

8. Make the frosting while the cookies are cooling. Whisk together the icing ingredients -in a small bowl. If the sauce is too thick, add a splash of lemon juice. If the mixture is too thin, -add a little more powdered sugar. Fill a Ziploc bag with the mixture, seal it, and cut a tiny hole in the corner tip. Drizzle the glaze over the cookies. The frosting will be hard enough to stack cookies on top of every other after it has set.

Almond Cranberry Cookies

Preparation Time: 12 minutes | Dehydrating Time: 6 hours

Servings: 4 to 6

Ingredients:

- 1 banana
- 1 tbsp honey
- Wet pulp from almond milk
- 2 tbsp coconut oil
- 1/2 cup almonds, coarsely chopped
- 3/4 cup shredded coconut flakes
- 1/2 cup dried cranberries

Directions:

1. In a food processor, mix all the ingredients. Place a small scoop of dough on dehydrator sheets and flatten it into a cookie.
2. Dehydrate for 6 hours at 105°F.

Cherry Coconut Almond Cookies

Preparation Time: 1 hour 20 minutes | Dehydrating time: 6 hours

Servings: 8

Ingredients:

- 1 cup salted almond butter
- 1 cup pitted dates (soaked in the water for 1/2 hour)
- 1 cup dried cherries (soaked in the water for 1/2 hour)
- 1 cup crushed almonds
- 1/8- 1/4 cup water
- 1 cup shredded coconut

Directions:

1. In a food processor, pulse the dried fruits. Add almond butter and crushed almonds. Pulse again.
2. Add in water slowly until the dough can be rolled into balls. Do not allow dough to get too runny. Flatten balls into discs and dip into shredded coconut to adhere to both sides.
3. Place on dehydrator sheet and set temperature to 145 degrees. Dehydrate for 3 hours and then flip over to other side for 3 hours.

☆ ☆ ☆ ☆ ☆

Carrot Cake

Preparation time: 30 minutes | Dehydrating time: 9 hours

Servings: 6

Ingredients:

- 3 cups carrots, grated
- 1 teaspoon cinnamon
- 1/2 teaspoon nutmeg
- 1/4 teaspoon ground cloves
- 1 cup pecans, crushed
- 1/2 cup shredded coconut
- 1/4 cup water
- 1/2 teaspoon salt

Directions:

1. In a food processor, mix the pecans and coconut and pulse.
2. In a large bowl, combine the carrots, pecans, coconut, cinnamon, nutmeg, cloves, water, and salt.
3. Place ParaFlexx Screens on the racks of your Food Dehydrator.
4. Form the dough into individual cakes about 4 inches across. Place the cakes onto the screens and set your Food dehydrator to 165F. Dehydrate for one hour, then lower the temperature to 125F and dehydrate for another 8 hours.

SOUPS

Cauliflower Soup

Preparation time: 40 minutes | Cooking time: 15 minutes

Servings: 4

Ingredients:

- 1/8 cup quinoa
- 4 cups vegetable stock
- pepper, to taste salt, to taste
- 2 cups dehydrated cauliflower
- 1/8 cup dehydrated onion
- 1/8 cup dehydrated celery
- 2 slices dehydrated garlic
- 2 1/2 cups water

Directions:

1. Cover cauliflower, onion, celery, and garlic with 212 cups boiling water in a large bowl. Soak vegetables for about 30 minutes, or until nearly rehydrated. Remove and dispose of the soaking liquid.
2. Add the vegetables, quinoa, vegetable stock, salt, pepper, and seasonings to taste in a large saucepan. 15 minutes over medium heat, until the cauliflower and quinoa are tender and fully cooked.
3. Remove from heat and blend in small batches using a blender. Be cautious; it will be extremely hot. 45 to 60 seconds are required for the blending procedure.

Asparagus Soup

Preparation time: 10 minutes | Cooking time: 20 minutes

Servings: 4

Ingredients:

- 1/2 teaspoon dried basil or 10 fresh basil leaves, chopped
- 4 cups chicken broth or stock
- 2 cups dehydrated asparagus
- 1 cup water
- 2 tablespoons butter or extra virgin olive oil
- salt and pepper, to taste

Directions:

1. Place the asparagus and water in a saucepan and simmer over medium heat for five to ten minutes, or until the asparagus is tender. Drain and save the liquid from asparagus.
2. About one minute after adding the asparagus, butter, and basil to a stockpot over medium heat, the butter will melt.
3. Add the chicken stock and asparagus water to the stockpot and bring the mixture to a boil over high heat. Reduce heat to low and simmer for ten minutes. Remove from heat and allow to cool for five minutes.
4. Warm soup is poured into a blender in small batches and pureed to the desired consistency. After pureeing, transfer small portions to a large bowl so that they remain distinct. So that the soup has texture, I like to leave a few blender batches with larger chunks.
5. Return mixture to the stockpot and season to taste with salt and pepper.

Vegetable Soup

Preparation time: 5 minutes | Cooking time: 4 hours

Servings: 4

Ingredients:

- pinch onion powder
- salt and pepper, to taste
- 1 tablespoon spaghetti, broken into small sections
- 1/3 cup dried vegetables
- 1/4 teaspoon dried parsley
- 1/4 teaspoon dried sweet basil pinch garlic powder
- 2 cups boiling chicken or beef broth

Directions:

1. Boil water and fill an empty Thermos with it. Pour the hot water out just prior to placing the ingredients in the Thermos.
2. In a Thermos, combine the dried vegetables, parsley, basil, garlic powder, onion powder, salt, pepper, and pasta.
3. Pour the chicken or beef broth that has been brought to a boil over the dry ingredients. Cover the Thermos quickly and securely. Shake or flip the Thermos every hour until mealtime, if possible.

Wilderness Stew

Preparation time: 40 minutes | Dehydrating time: 6 hours

Servings: 4

Ingredients:

- 1 Pound Ground Beef
- 1 Can Black Beans

- 1 Container of Black Beans
- Diced Potatoes, Two
- 1 Red Pepper Finely Diced
- 1 Green Pepper Diced
- 1 Onion Chop
- 5 Tomaotes
- A pinch of salt
- 2 Liters Water

Directions:

1. In a large saucepan, sear the meat.
2. Add water, bell peppers, onion, potatoes, and tomatoes to the pan.
3. Bring to a boil, then decrease heat to a simmer for ten minutes.
4. Add salt and beans to taste.
5. Bring back to a boil and simmer for two minutes.
6. Cool, then serve and enjoy.

Tomato and Seafood Chowder

Preparation time: 10 minutes | Dehydrating Time: 8 hours

Servings: 4

Ingredients:

- 2 tablespoons tomato sauce powder
- 1/2 teaspoon vegetable soup base
- 1 teaspoon fish seasoning for flavor
- 1 tablespoon dehydrated shrimp
- 1 tablespoon dehydrated, canned mussel
- 1 tablespoon shelf-stable imitation crab meat

Storage: Everything can be sealed together in a bag for consumption on-trail. Nothing needs to be stored separately, making this particularly appealing.

To Rehydrate:

1. Place everything into a pot along with 1 1/4 cups of water. Bring to a boil and stir. Lower heat and simmer for 5 minutes, or until everything is hot and rehydrated.
2. Enjoy!

Lentil Curry

Preparation time: 10 minutes | Dehydrating Time: 8 hours

Servings: 4

Ingredients:

- 1/2 cup cooked, dehydrated lentils
- 1 tablespoon curry powder
- 1 tablespoon dehydrated carrots
- 1 tablespoon dehydrated corn
- 1 tablespoon dehydrated peas
- 1 tablespoon dehydrated peppers
- 1 teaspoon coconut oil (optional)

Directions:

1. Combine everything but oil in one bag. Keep oil separate.

To Rehydrate:

1. Boil 1 cup of water, and add it to a boil-in bag. Mix and let sit 15 minutes, or until vegetables and lentils are tender. Add more water if needed, but don't oversaturate your lentils. Top with coconut oil and stir again before eating.

Beef Bell Pepper Soup

Preparation Time: 15 minutes | Dehydrating time: 30 minutes

Servings: 6

Ingredients:

- 1/2 cup freeze-dried ground beef
- 3/4 cup instant brown rice
- 1/4 cup dried celery
- 1/3 cup dehydrated sliced onion
- 1 cup dehydrated bell peppers
- 1 tablespoon beef bouillon
- 1 teaspoon garlic powder
- 3/4 cup tomato powder
- 1/4 cup freeze dried sausage crumbled
- 9 cups water

Directions:

1. Add all ingredients except water into the glass jar. Seal jar tightly with lid.
2. To Dehydrating time: Add water and jar content to the saucepan and bring to boil.
3. Reduce heat and simmer for 15-20 minutes.
4. Serve and enjoy.

DAIRY

Dehydrated Milk Powder

Preparation time: 10 minutes | Dehydrating time: 10 hours

Servings: 40

Ingredients:

- 8 cups whole milk

Directions:

1. Set the temperature of your dehydrator to 135°F.
2. Line the dehydrator trays with parchment paper.
3. Fold the corners of parchment paper and then secure each folded corner with a clip, creating a square bowl.
4. Carefully pour the milk onto the dehydrator trays in a thin layer.
5. Dehydrate for about 10 hours.
6. Remove from dehydrator and set aside to cool completely.
7. Into a clean food processor, add the dried milk and pulse on a high setting until finely powdered.
8. You can preserve this milk powder in airtight glass containers at room temperature for up to 2 months.

Dehydrated Buttermilk Powder

Preparation time: 10 minutes | Dehydrating time: 5 hours

Servings: 4

Ingredients

- 3 cups buttermilk

Directions:

1. Set the temperature of your dehydrator to 135°F.

2. Line the dehydrator trays with parchment paper.
3. Fold the corners of parchment paper and then secure each folded corner with a clip, creating a square bowl.
4. Carefully pour the milk onto the dehydrator trays in a thin layer
5. Dehydrate for about 4-5 hours.
6. Remove from dehydrator and set aside to cool completely.
7. In a clean food processor, add the dried buttermilk and pulse on a high setting until finely powdered.
8. You can preserve this buttermilk powder in airtight glass containers at room temperature for up to 3 months.

Cheese Powder

Preparation Time: 20 minutes | Dehydration Time: 15 hours

Servings: 2

Ingredients:

- 1 block hard cheese (Parmesan, Gruyere, Cheddar), sliced

Directions:

1. Add the cheese slices to the Cosori Premium Food Dehydrator.
2. Process at 145 degrees F for 15 hours.
3. Transfer the dehydrated cheese to a food processor.
4. Pulse until powdery.

Storage Suggestions: Store the cheese powder in a large spice bottle. Keep refrigerated.

Preparation & Dehydration Tips: Slice the cheese as thinly as possible to dehydrate faster.

Powdered Cheese

Preparation Time: 20 minutes | Dehydration Time: 10 hours

Servings: 2

Ingredients:

- 1 block of any cheese

Directions:

1. To prepare the cheese, finely grate it to help it dry faster.
2. Lay the cheese out evenly on the tray of the dehydrator.
3. Dry the cheese at 125 degrees Fahrenheit for 8-12 hours.
4. Check on the cheese and blot any excess oil with a paper towel when necessary.
5. Let it cool and remove it from the dehydrator.
6. Grind the cheese into a powder using a food processor.
7. Sift the powder through a sieve & store in a sealed container.

Yogurt

Preparation Time: 20 minutes | Dehydration Time: 8 hours

Servings: 2

Ingredients:

- 1 quart milk
- 2 tablespoons cultured yogurt

Directions:

1. In a saucepan, heat the milk to 180 degrees Fahrenheit. It will start to froth at this temperature.
2. Remove from heat and let the milk cool to 120 degrees Fahrenheit.
3. Add in the cultured yogurt.

4. Lay the yogurt out evenly on the tray of the dehydrator.

5. Dry the yogurt at 110 degrees Fahrenheit for 9 hours.

6. Let it cool and remove it from the dehydrator.

7. Strain the yogurt until it has thickened.

8. Store it in a sealed container in the refrigerator.

Ground Cottage Cheese

Preparation Time: 15 minutes | Dehydration Time: 15 hours

Servings: 1

Ingredients:

- 2 cups cottage cheese

Directions:

1. Spread the cottage cheese in the Cosori Premium Food Dehydrator.

2. Dry at 145 degrees F for 15 hours.

Storage Suggestions: Store in an airtight and watertight glass jar with lid.

Preparation & Dehydration Tips: You can also use other soft cheeses for this recipe.

Yogurt Leather

Preparation Time: 15 minutes | Dehydration Time: 8 hours

Servings: 3

Ingredients:

- 3 cups yogurt

Directions:

1. Spread the yogurt in the Cosori Premium Food Dehydrator.
2. Process at 125 degrees F for 8 hours.

Storage Suggestions: Slice into strips. Wrap each strip with waxed paper.

Preparation & Dehydration Tips: Sprinkle with sugar if you want to sweet it a bit.

FLOUR

Raw Herb and Seed Bread

Preparation Time 30 minutes | Dehydrating time 16 hours

Servings: 4

Ingredients:

- 2/3 cup flax seeds Sunflower seeds
- 1/3 cup a third cup of minced onion Carrots, grated, in a cup
- 2 to 3 minced garlic cloves
- 1 TBL dry herbs or 1/3 cup chopped fresh herbs
- Sesame seeds, 1/4 cup
- 2 TBL of soy sauce
- When required, water

Directions:

1. Sunflower and flax seeds should be combined in a blender. To a mixing basin, add the remaining ingredients (except the water)
2. Completely combine.
3. 1 TBL at a time; as needed, add water. You want a batter that can be easily spread on your dehydrator sheet and is moist but not runny.
4. It should be spread out on a Teflex sheet on your dehydrator tray.
5. Using the back of a spoon, spread it evenly across the sheet.
6. Dehydrate for 8–10 hours at 110 °F or until the reflex layer comes off.
7. Flip the bread over and remove the reflex layer. Turn the bread over and keep drying it if it starts to crumble.
8. Dehydrate the bread for a further 6 to 8 hours or until the proper texture is restored.
9. Bread should be cut into serving-size squares.
10. For up to a week, store chilled in an airtight container.

Raw Zucchini Bread

Preparation Time: 20 minutes | Dehydrating time: 6 hours

Servings: 6

Ingredients:

- 2 cups Walnuts
- 2 teaspoons Cinnamon
- 1 1/2 cup Dates
- 1 teaspoon Vanilla Extract
- 3 cups Grated Zucchini
- 1 cup Shredded Unsweetened Coconut
- 1/2 cup Raisins
- 1/2 cup Psyllium Husk

Directions:

1. Add the walnuts to your food processor and pulse until ground. Add the cinnamon, dates, and vanilla and process until combined. Transfer to a bowl, add the zucchini, coconut, raisins, and psyllium husk and mix well to combine. Use the mixture to make 10 loaves and place them on the dehydrator trays lined with parchment paper. Dehydrate at 150F/65C for an hour, reduce the temperature to 110F/43C and dehydrate for 5 more hours. When done, allow to cool and store in the fridge.

Black Bread

Preparation time: 30 minutes | Dehydrating time: 8 to 12 hours

Servings: 4

Ingredients:

- 2 Garlic Cloves, peeled
- 1/4 cup Water
- 1 teaspoon Lemon Juice
- 1/4 cup Chopped Red Onion
- 1 tablespoon Agave Nectar
- 1 tablespoon Cacao Powder
- 1/4 cup Ground Flax Seeds
- 1 tablespoon Caraway seeds
- 1/4 teaspoon Black Pepper
- 1 cup Raw Walnuts, soaked overnight, rinsed and drained
- 1 cup Buckwheat Groats, soaked overnight, rinsed and drained

Directions:

1. Add the walnuts and buckwheat groats to your blender or food processor and pulse until chopped. Add the garlic, water, lemon juice, onion, and agave nectar and pulse until combined.
2. Transfer to a medium bowl then mix in the cacao, flaxseed meal, caraway seeds, and pepper.
3. Pour the dough onto a dehydrator sheet, spread it until it is ¼-inch thick and score it into squares or rectangles.
4. Dehydrate at 115F / 46C for 8 to 12 depending on the preferred doneness.
5. When done, break into pieces and store in airtight containers.

Vanilla Wheat Cereal

Preparation Time: 12 hours | Dehydrating time: 12 hours

Servings: 6

Ingredients:

- 6 cups buckwheat
- 1 1/2 tablespoons vanilla concentrate
- 2 cups applesauce
- 1 tablespoon cinnamon
- 1 teaspoon allspice
- 2 teaspoons salt

Directions:

1. In a huge bowl, splash the buckwheat for 12 hours and drain.
2. In a food processor, add the buckwheat, vanilla, fruit purée, cinnamon, allspice, and salt. Beat until the combination frames a free paste. Place ParaFlexx Screens on the racks of your Food dehydrator and spread the blend equitably on the screens.
3. Set your Food dehydrator to 115F and get dried out for 12 hours or until totally dried. Eliminate the cereal from the racks and break into little pieces. Store in a hermetically sealed container.

Chocolate Chip Pumpkin Bread

Preparation Time: 10 Min | Cooking Time: 1 Hr 0 Min

Servings: 2 Loaves

Ingredients:

- 3 cups of + 1 tbsp all-purpose flour, divided

- 1 tbsp + 2 tsp pumpkin pie spice
- 2 tsp baking soda
- 1 1/2 tsp salt
- 3 cups of granulated sugar
- 1 can (15 oz) LIBBY'S® 100% Pure Pumpkin
- 4 large eggs
- 1 cup of vegetable oil
- 1/2 cup of orange- juice or water
- 1 1/4 cups of NESTLÉ TOLL HOUSE® Semi-Sweet Chocolate Morsels

Directions:

1. Preheat the oven to 350 degrees Fahrenheit. Two 9 x 5-inch loaf pans should be greased and floured.

2. In a large mixing basin, mix 3 cups of flour, pumpkin pie spice, baking soda, and salt. In a large mixer bowl, -mix the sugar, pumpkin, eggs, oil, and juice; beat until just mixd. Stir just til the flour mixture is wet with the pumpkin mixture. Toss the morsels with the remaining 1 tbsp flour before folding them into the batter. Pour the batter -into the loaf pans that have been prepped.

3. Bake for 60–65 mins, or til a wooden pick inserted in the middle comes out clean. Cool for 10 minutesin pans on wire racks before removing to wire racks to cool fully.

Pumpkin Flour

Preparation Time: 15 minutes | Dehydration Time: 8 hours

Servings: 2

Ingredients:

- 4 cups pumpkin puree

Directions:

1. Spread the pureed pumpkin in the Cosori Premium Food Dehydrator.
2. Process at 125 degrees F for 8 hours.
3. Transfer to a coffee grinder.
4. Grind until powdery.
5. Storage Suggestions: Store in an airtight jar for up to 5 years.
6. Preparation & Dehydration Tips: You can also use pureed squash for this recipe.

Corn Flour

Preparation Time: 15 minutes | Dehydration Time: 12 hours

Servings: 2

Ingredients:

- 8 cups corn kernels

Directions:

1. Spread the corn kernels in the Cosori Premium Food Dehydrator.
2. Process at 145 degrees F for 12 hours.
3. Transfer the dried corn in a food processor or coffee grinder.
4. Grind until powdery.
5. Storage Suggestions: Store the flour in an airtight glass jar.
6. Preparation & Dehydration Tips: Do not overcrowd the dehydrator. If necessary, process the corn kernels by batch.

OTHER RECIPES

Dehydrated Apple Cinnamon Quinoa Porridge

Preparation Time: 20 minutes | Dehydrating Time: 8 hours

Servings: 5

Ingredients:

- one cup quinoa sliced into 1/2" cubes, two apples
- 2 glasses of water
- 1 teaspoon of cinnamon
- 14 teaspoon salt
- Maple syrup, 1/4 cup
- 1/4 cup of coconut milk powder and
- 1 teaspoon vanilla essence
- 12 cups of pecans, chopped

Directions

1. Rinse quinoa in a fine-mesh sieve until clear. Apples, water, cinnamon, and salt in a saucepan. Reduce heat after boiling and cover. Cooking quinoa takes 15-20 minutes. Salt, pepper, maple syrup, and vanilla.
2. Spread quinoa on dehydrator trays. Dehydrate quinoa and apples at 135°F for 8 to 12 hours.

On-Trail Planning

1. In a cookpot, combine the quinoa and 8 ounces of water for each serving to make it while camping. Stirring occasionally, cook the quinoa for the specified amount of time on low heat.

Dehydrated Rice

Preparation time: 5 minutes | Dehydrating time: 6 hrs

Servings: 5

Ingredients

- 1 cup uncooked rice
- 1-1/2 to 2 cups of water or low-fat or no-fat broth
- 1-2 teaspoon salt

Directions

1. Rice should be thoroughly rinsed until the water is clear.
2. White rice requires 1 1/2 cups of water, brown rice 2 cups.
3. Salt the rice and then incorporate. For white rice, cover the pan and cook for 18–20 minutes; for brown rice, simmer for 35–40 minutes (or as indicated on the package). TRAIL TIP: For best results, err on the side of slightly overcooked rice rather than uncooked rice while rehydrating on the trail.
4. Rice can cool more quickly if any excess starch is washed away with running water. Drain completely.
5. On the drying trays that have been prepared, evenly distribute the rice in a single layer. Liners will prevent little kernels from falling through the mesh while the rice dries.
6. Dry at 125°F (52°C) for six to eight hours. The humidity level and the type of rice affect how long it takes for rice to dry.
7. While monitoring the rice's drying, break up any clumps that form to ensure even drying.
8. The rice is prepared for consumption when it is translucent and firm all throughout.
9. Give the trays cooling time an hour.
10. Break up any large clumps for the best quality, and store them for up to 6 months in a glass jar. For longer shelf life, use oxygen absorbers, vacuum seal, and keep in a cold, dark

location. The longer shelf life of brown rice is a result of its higher fat content.

11. Dry rice can be used on its own or in dehydrated dishes such as Red Thai Curry, Brown Rice Porridge, Ham and Rice, Fiesta Rice, and others.

12. 1 plate of rice after rehydrating (about 1 cup of cooked rice)

13. Boil 1 cup of water. 2/3 cup rice. Cover and cook until liquid evaporates and rice is mushy 12 to 15 minutes.

14. Return to the heat if required to warm up.

15. A final volume of 1 to 1 1/4 cups of completed, cooked rice may result from rehydrating white rice for 12 minutes as opposed to 15 minutes for brown rice.

16. ☆ ☆ ☆ ☆ ☆

Homemade Tea with Rose and Dried Fruit

Preparation Time: 20 minutes | Dehydrating time: 12 hours

Servings: 5

Ingredients

- Dehydrate 1 1/2 lbs of each fresh fruit (strawberries, apples, and oranges) and save the leftovers.
- 1 1/2 cups of dried organic oranges
- 1 1/2 cups of dried organic apples
- 1 1/2 cups dried organic strawberries
- 1 1/2 cups of dried organic rose petals
- White tea, two cups

Directions

1. Use a vegetable brush to scrub the oranges and apples, then give them a good rinse. It's important to thoroughly clean and drains strawberries. Dry the fruit surface with a paper towel.

2. Fruits should be sliced crosswise using a sharp knife. Slice the

fruit into 14-inch-thick pieces while leaving the peel on. Slice ends ought to be thrown away.

3. The fruit slices should then be arranged on the dehydrator trays. Turn on the dehydrator and insert the trays.

4. Dehydrate the fruit slices afterward until the fruit center is completely dry. Depending on how many trays are piled, this might take anywhere from six to eight hours.

5. To ensure that the slices dry evenly, don't forget to rotate the trays.

6. After the fruit slices have been properly dried and crisped, cut them into smaller pieces.

Camping Egg Breakfast

Preparation Time: 20 minutes | Dehydrating time: 8 to 10 hours

Servings: 5

Ingredients:

- 5 eggs, large

Directions:

1. Crack the eggs in a bowl. You may need to split the amount for the size of your dehydrator trays.

2. Whisk eggs well, till blended fully and a bit foamy.

3. Carefully pour eggs into fruit leather dehydrator tray.

4. Dehydrate the eggs at 140F for 8 – 10 hours till flaky and fully dried. The egg flakes will be oily, so it should be easy to scrape them away without them sticking to tray when they have fully dried. If your eggs still feel sticky, leave sticky eggs in dehydrator for a short additional time period.

5. Transfer the dried egg flakes to zipper top plastic bag. Place in the freezer for 1/2 to 1 full hour.

6. Remove the eggs from the freezer. Blend in your food processor till fully powdered. They should not stick to food processor sides at all. If they do, they need to dry more. Put eggs in dehydrator again if they need more drying.

7. Store the eggs in a zipper lock plastic bag in a freezer till ready for use.

Pumpkin Lovers' Pancakes

Preparation Time: 10 minutes | Dehydrating time: 15 minutes

Servings: 1

Ingredients:

- 3 & 1/2 ounces of batter mix, pancake
- 2 tablespoons of pumpkin powder
- To fry: ghee (clarified butter)

Directions:

1. Combine the mixture of pancake batter with pumpkin powder in zipper top plastic bag.
2. Pack the ghee separately. Store till ready to use.

Dehydrated Eggs

Preparation Time: 5 minutes | Dehydrating Time: 10 hours

Servings: 4

Ingredients:

- 5 eggs

Directions:

1. Separate eggs into separate bowls. The number of eggs I can most easily fit into one of my dehydrator trays is five. Adjust according to the specifications of your dehydrator and egg requirements, dividing the mixture among many trays if necessary.

2. The eggs should be whisked very well until they are completely combined and have a small bit of foam on top.

3. It is important to ensure that the dehydrator is put on a level surface before proceeding with the next step, carefully pouring the eggs onto the fruit leather tray of the dehydrator.

4. You should dehydrate eggs for eight to ten hours at a temperature of 140°F until they are dried and flaky.

5. Egg flakes are oily, and after they are completely dried, they should be easy to scrape from the tray without leaving any residue. If they are still sticky, the sticky part should be left in the oven for a little longer.

6. Set the dried egg flakes in a baggie with a zip-top closure, and then place the baggie in the freezer for 30 minutes to 1 hour.

7. Take the eggs out of the freezer and mix them in a food processor or blender until they are pulverized entirely. They are not dry enough if they stick to the pan's sides. Placed once again within the dehydrator for an additional period.

8. Keep it in the freezer in a baggie with a zip-top closure until your camping trip.

CONCLUSION

Thank you for reading this cookbook. Food dehydration is an ancient method of preserving food for longer periods of time. It could be a replacement for freezing or canning, or it could complement those methods.

Dehydrated foods are simple, safe, and easy to prepare. Dehydration is one of the earliest food storage techniques, and techniques for drying food have also advanced over time. Food dehydration at home is an easy way for many people to save food.

Using this simple and effective method, you will be able to store food that is not only efficient but also tasty, portable, and long-lasting. These are the qualities you want in dangerous situations. There isn't much equipment needed, and most of it is either already in your possession or can be obtained for a low cost. Dry meals contain so little moisture that the organisms that cause food to spoil cannot live in them. This is the key to dry foods' success.

If you want to keep your food, change your snack game, or plan a future hiking trip, dehydrating your food is simple and satisfying. The drying process gradually removes excess water while preserving nutrition and flavor. This may also be less expensive and healthier than pre-cooked meals, which is important for travelers looking to save space and weight.

www.ingramcontent.com/pod-product-compliance
Lightning Source LLC
Chambersburg PA
CBHW061004050726
47592CB00003B/1346